IN THE BEGINNING

Olayiwola Michael

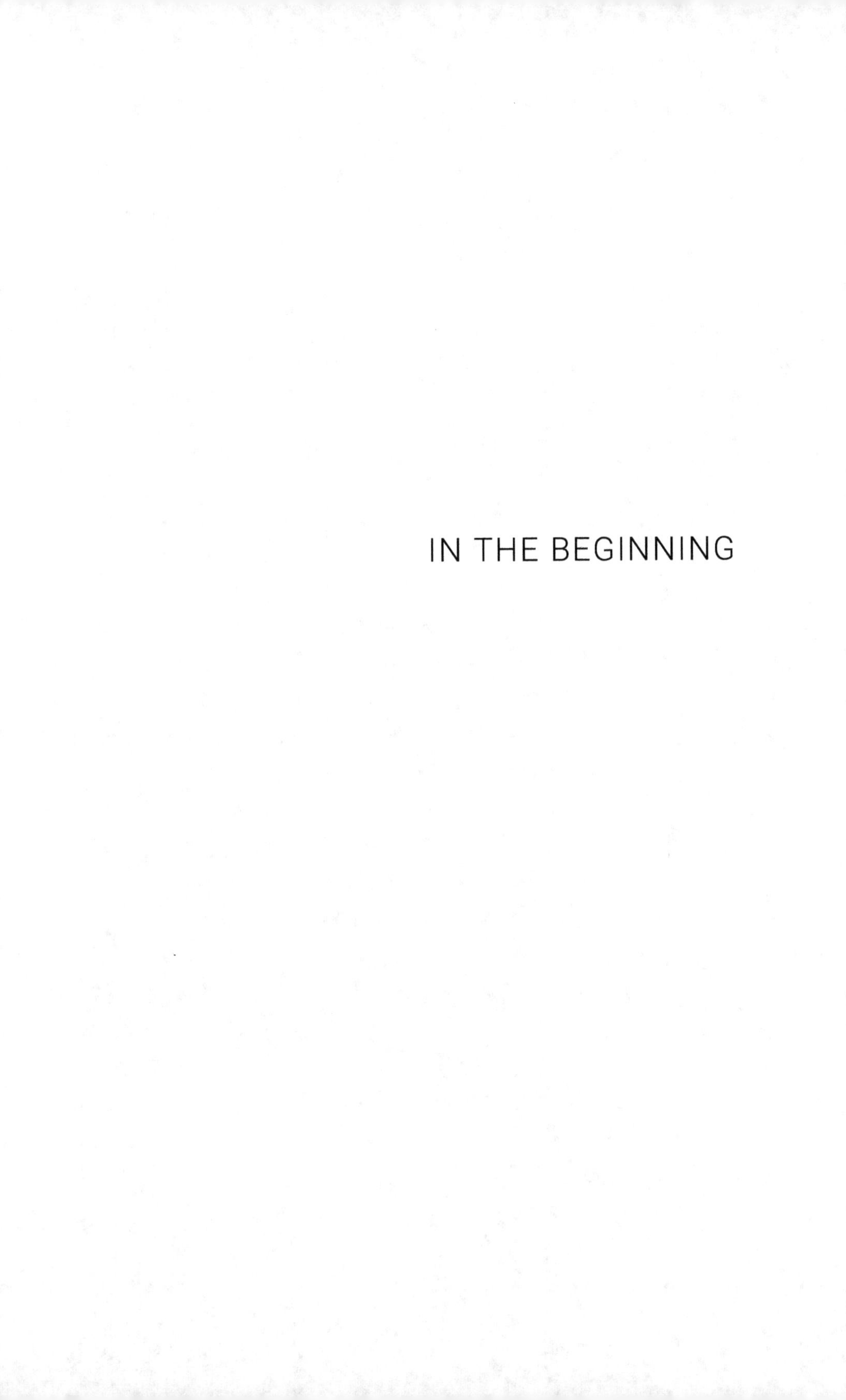

IN THE BEGINNING

In the Beginning is a theological exploration of the importance of beginnings in our relationship with God. The book uses biblical narratives and parables to illustrate how our initial commitment to God, marked by faith, passion, and dedication, lays the foundation for our spiritual growth. It warns against the dangers of straying from this initial commitment, highlighting how worldly distractions and Satan's temptations can lead us astray. The book emphasizes the need for vigilance, self-reflection, and a constant return to God's word to maintain a strong and fulfilling relationship with Him. It encourages readers to remember their beginnings, rekindle their first love for God, and stay rooted in His truth to experience the fullness of His blessings.

Emphasizing the Importance of Beginnings

Genesis 1:1 says, "In the beginning, God created the heavens and the earth." This verse highlights that there is a beginning to all creation, suggesting that nothing exists without an underlying foundation or starting point.

The book of Genesis in the Bible describes the origins and creation of the universe, according to the Judeo-Christian tradition. The text details how God created the world, including humanity, and even the figure of Satan. The book of Genesis illustrates how some beginnings or origins can lead to glory and prosperity, while others may result in destruction and adversity, as depicted through the various narratives in this biblical text.

For example, the book of Ruth shows how Ruth's beginning with Naomi was good, but her latter end was even greater. Ruth 3:10 states, "Blessed be thou of the Lord, my daughter: for thou hast showed more kindness in the latter end than at the beginning, inasmuch as thou followedst not young men, whether poor or rich." This highlights how Ruth's faithfulness and kindness to Naomi increased over time, resulting in a greater outcome.

Similarly, our relationship with God should follow a trajectory of growth and development. Genesis 1:1 tells us that God created everything good in the beginning, including Adam and Eve. However, their disobedience and deception by Satan led to the departure of God's beauty and glory from their lives. This should make us reflect on the state of our relationship with God, too.

Just as children start with the basics in school, our journey with God begins with learning the fundamentals of faith. However, some may struggle to remain focused, while others may progress more easily. Ultimately, our path should lead us to deeper obedience and alignment with God's ways, as we seek to continue believing in Him and His Son, Jesus.

Unfortunately, not everyone who encounters Jesus and witnesses His miracles chooses to believe. John 10:24-27 highlights how some Jews doubted and did not believe, despite the evidence of Jesus's divine power and anointing. This serves as a warning that even in the face of undeniable proof, some may still reject the truth.

The message here is to not forget our beginning in the kingdom of God and to remain faithful to our first love. All the steps God wants us to follow, the way He wants us to live, and how He wants us to relate to Him, must be in tune with His Word, guiding us until our last day on earth.

As we eagerly await the return of our Lord Jesus Christ, we should be ready to die and give our lives for Him, just as the apostles did. This motivated their unwavering commitment and fearless service, which should inspire us to remain steadfast in our beginning with Christ, avoiding the path of doubt and deviation. Ruth did not deviate from the path, but she remained on it until glory came. Enduring and increasing in character over time. Are you increasing in righteousness and character?

For a true believer in God, destined for eternal life, following the truth of God's word should not be overly difficult. However, for those who are not predestined for salvation, the truth of God's teachings may always pose a challenge for them. This dynamic is illustrated in the Gospel of John, chapter 10, where Jesus encounters both those who accept his message and those who reject it.

When the truth of God's word comes to a true child of God, the appropriate response is self-examination. The believer should look within themselves to identify any areas that need correction or amendment to fully align with God's truth. Once identified, the believer should then make the necessary changes to bring their life into closer conformity with the truth.

The key distinction is between those who are ordained by God for eternal life, and thus receptive to God's truth, versus those who are not, and thus tend to struggle with or resist the truth. For the true believer, the response should be humble self-reflection and adherence to God's ways.

Just like Ruth, you too can increase in character. Your beginning is crucial because it lays the foundation for your life, such as when you gave your life to Jesus and began to walk in God's truth. There is nothing that was created that does not have a beginning.

Everything in life follows a natural progression. Just as we learn by starting with the basics and gradually moving towards more complex concepts, so too did God create the world in stages.

Think of education: We begin in preschool, building a foundation of basic skills. Then, we progress through kindergarten, elementary, middle school, and finally university, each stage adding new knowledge and understanding. We can't skip ahead; each step is essential.

Similarly, God's creation unfolded in stages. He didn't just snap his fingers and do everything at once. He carefully crafted the world, starting with the foundations and gradually adding complexity. Man, as the pinnacle of creation, came last.

Up until the events in Genesis Chapter 3, everything God made was perfect and good. It was only with the introduction of deception that things changed, marking a shift in the harmony of creation.

Eve was convinced by Satan to ignore God's commandments, and she then convinced her husband as well. God may have told you not to marry a certain person, but the Devil persuaded you to do so. God may have told you to run, but Satan told you to stand. God may have instructed you to write, but the Devil directed you to do something else. This is how he deceives God's children until they are destroyed and rejected by God, which is his goal. He makes them forget their beginnings.

In the beginning of their relationship with God, many people prayed diligently or found time to pray daily. However, they suddenly became lukewarm, no longer having time to read His word or fellowship with Him. Some even stopped going to church, unaware that this abnormal behavior was caused by satanic power.

Satan is cunning and will use any means to weaken our faith. One of his favorite tactics is to exploit our physical weaknesses, like tiredness, to distract us from our spiritual lives.

Here's how to recognize and overcome this tactic:

The Tiredness Trap: Excessive yawning could be more than just physical fatigue; it might be a sign that Satan is trying to discourage your prayer life. His goal is to make you give in to tiredness, neglect your connection with God, and become distracted from the important tasks you are working on or trying to complete.

Fight Back with Fasting and Prayer: Don't let tiredness win! Instead, see it as a call to action. Fast and pray, even if it's just for a short period, focusing on the weariness and seeking God's strength.

Listen for God's Guidance: As you pray, be attentive to God's voice. He may reveal the root cause of your tiredness and offer guidance on how to overcome it.

Guard Your Foundations: Remember that this new wave of weariness could be a tactic to make you fall away from your initial commitment to God. Be vigilant and constantly strive to maintain the same level of dedication and intimacy you had at the beginning of your relationship with Him.

By recognizing Satan's tactics and actively fighting back with prayer and fasting, you can overcome these challenges and strengthen your relationship with God. Remember, He is always with you, ready to provide the strength and guidance you need.

Just like a marriage, our relationship with God can evolve over time. The initial spark and intensity might fade, and the path we walk together might change, either for the better or for the worse.

The key to a healthy and fulfilling relationship with God, just as in a marriage, is to remember our beginnings. Recall the passion, the commitment, the unwavering faith we had when we first encountered Him.

This remembrance serves as a guiding light, leading us back to the source of our joy and strength. It reminds us of the powerful bond we share with God and inspires us to rekindle that flame.

Just as couples who remember the early days of their love are more likely to navigate challenges and maintain a strong connection, so too can we strengthen our relationship with God by remembering the foundation upon which it was built.

The story of Solomon serves as a cautionary tale for us all. He began his reign with a heart devoted to God, seeking wisdom and guidance. Yet, over time, he allowed the allure of worldly pleasures and the influence of his many wives to draw him away from his commitment to the Lord.

This pattern of falling away from God, once having a strong foundation, is sadly common today. Just as Adam and Eve were deceived by the serpent, many are lured by the lies and temptations of the world, choosing to believe the Devil's whispers over God's truth.

Think of the parable of the Sower: The seed represents the word of God, and the different types of soil represent different responses to that word. Some hearts, like the rocky ground, receive the word with enthusiasm but lack deep roots, quickly falling away when faced with challenges. Others, like the thorny ground, become entangled with worldly cares and distractions, choking out the growth of faith.

Remembering our beginnings is crucial to staying on the path of righteousness. It reminds us of the initial passion, the pure desire to follow God, and the joy we experienced in His presence.

Here's how to stay true to your beginnings:

Guard Your Heart: Be mindful of the influences in your life. Choose friends who encourage your faith, seek godly counsel, and be discerning about the information you consume.

Stay Rooted in God's Word: Regularly read and study the Bible, allowing it to shape your thoughts and actions.

Don't Be Deceived: Be aware of the enemy's tactics and resist his attempts to lure you away from God.

Remember Your First Love: Recall the joy and peace you felt when you first encountered God. Let that memory fuel your commitment to Him.

Just as Solomon's story serves as a warning, it also offers hope. We can choose to resist the temptations that led him astray and remain steadfast in our commitment to God. By remembering our beginnings, we can stay on the path of righteousness and experience the fullness of God's blessings.

2

Reasons for Lack of Spiritual Fruitfulness

According to the parable of the Sower in the Bible, there are several reasons why some people did not produce spiritual fruits:

Lack of Understanding (Matthew 13:19):
When anyone hears the word of the kingdom but does not understand it, the evil one comes and snatches away what was sown in his/her heart. Without comprehending the true meaning and significance of the word, it cannot take root and bear fruit.

Lack of Depth/Commitment (Matthew 13:20-21):
The seed falling on rocky ground refers to someone who hears the word and at once receives it with joy. However, because they have no firm root system. When trouble or persecution arises because of the word, they quickly fall away, as their commitment is shallow.

Preoccupation with Worldly Concerns (Matthew 13:22):
The seed falling among the thorns refers to someone who hears the word, but the worries of this life and the deceitfulness of wealth choke the word, making it unfruitful. Worldly anxieties and the allure of material possessions can distract and hinder one's spiritual growth.

In summary, the parable emphasizes the importance of truly hearing, understanding, and wholeheartedly embracing the word of God. It also highlights the need to maintain this commitment in the face of trials and temptations to bear spiritual fruit. As stated in Matthew 13:23, "But he that received seed into the good ground is he that heareth the word, and understandeth it; which also beareth fruit, and bringeth forth, some an hundredfold, some sixty, some thirty."

Satan desires to disrupt our lives, including our businesses, relationships, and relationship with God. That is why we must be vigilant and ensure that our actions and decisions are rooted in the truth of God's word. When we notice troubling signs in our lives, we must address them promptly, lest they take root and lead us astray.

The journey of faith, like any journey, begins with a starting point. From the creation narrative in Genesis to the stories of Ruth and Solomon, the Bible consistently underscores the significance of our beginnings. Just as a building's foundation determines its stability, our initial commitment to God sets the course for our spiritual growth and endurance.

This chapter has explored the importance of remembering our beginnings, not as a nostalgic exercise, but as a vital tool for navigating the challenges of life. We've seen how forgetting our roots can lead to a decline in faith, just as Solomon's pursuit of worldly pleasures overshadowed his initial devotion to God. We've also examined the parable of the Sower, which highlights the various obstacles that can hinder spiritual growth, including a lack of understanding, shallow commitment, and the distractions of worldly concerns.

The key takeaway is that a strong foundation, built on a deep understanding of God's word and a steadfast commitment to His will, is essential for bearing spiritual fruit. This foundation is not static; it requires constant nurturing through prayer, study, and fellowship. It also demands vigilance against the deceptive tactics of Satan, who seeks to weaken our faith and lead us astray.

As we continue our journey, let us remember the words of Naomi to Ruth: "Blessed be thou of the Lord, my daughter: for thou hast showed more kindness in the latter end than at the beginning."

May we strive to grow in our faith, deepen our understanding of God's truth, and strengthen our commitment to Him. May we never forget the joy and peace we experienced in our initial encounter with God, allowing that memory to guide us through every trial and temptation. For in remembering our beginnings, we find the strength to endure, the wisdom to navigate, and the grace to grow into the image of Christ.

3

The Importance of Wisdom and the Fear of the Lord

Proverbs 1:7 states, "The fear of the Lord is the beginning of knowledge, but fools despise wisdom and instruction." This verse highlights a crucial truth: true knowledge begins with a deep respect and reverence for God.

When we fear the Lord, we become stronger in resisting the Devil's temptations. The Devil often tries to entice us into sin, especially through the desire for things we don't have. But when we are impatient and ignore wisdom, we become more vulnerable. These traits can lead to poor decisions and pull us away from God's plan for our lives.

Gehazi's story serves as a powerful reminder. He initially fell into sin and suffered the consequences, but ultimately received God's forgiveness and restoration. This story teaches us that even when we stumble, God desires to see us stand firm in His truth.

The Lord wants us to live lives that reflect His kingdom, bearing the fruits of the Spirit and fulfilling the purpose He has for us. He calls us to remember our beginnings and to seek His guidance in every aspect of our lives.

The passage from Revelation 2:1-5 demonstrates how forgetting one's spiritual beginnings can lead to destruction. In this passage, God addresses the church in Ephesus, commending them for their works, labor, and perseverance, but also rebuking them for having left their "first love."

God exhorts the Ephesian believers to "remember from where you have fallen, and repent and do the first works." In other words, they are to recall their initial devotion and commitment to Christ and return to that foundational relationship. Straying from one's spiritual beginning, simply going along with the crowd, and forsaking the fear and reverence of God, can lead to a dangerous spiritual decline.

As Proverbs 1:7 states, "The fear of the Lord is the beginning of knowledge, but fools despise wisdom and instruction." Disregarding the truth and prioritizing self-interest over obedience to God is the height of foolishness. The Jews in John 10:24 exemplify this, as they doubted and resisted Jesus despite the clear evidence of his identity and authority.

The emphasis on "the beginning" is crucial. God created mankind in His own image to have dominion over the earth and live in eternal fellowship with Him. However, when people reject this foundational truth and purpose, they risk losing eternal life and the ability to truly live as God intended. As John 10:27 affirms, Christ's sheep hear and follow His voice - the beginning of a life-giving relationship with the Good Shepherd.

The Bible's consistent message is that the starting point, the foundation, is vitally important. In Proverbs 8:22, we read that "The Lord possessed me at the beginning of his work." God's creative and redemptive work began with a perfect design, and He desires for His people to remain grounded in that initial vision and purpose.

Ultimately, the admonition is clear: do not forget your spiritual beginnings. Maintain the fear of the Lord, the love of Christ, and the understanding of your created purpose. Avoid the dangerous temptation to stray from the path of righteousness, and instead, return to the solid foundation that God has laid from the very start.

I am still on the subject named "In the beginning," Let's get this understanding - the Bible teaches us that God created everything perfectly for us from the start. This is a very important truth for us to learn and understand. We need to come to the fullness of God's understanding.

The "beginning" is foundational, as it is the starting point of creation and life. When you are born, when you start school, when you embark on a new chapter - these are all new beginnings. And in each new beginning, there are stories, challenges, and growth opportunities.

However, it is also in these new beginnings that we can stray from God's guidance and instructions. This can lead us down a path of self-reliance and destruction, rather than one of God's blessing and empowerment.

For example, a young person may decide to pursue wealth and status rather than seek God's will. While this may seem appealing, it ultimately leads away from the beauty and glory of God's plan. We have seen many lives ruined by this kind of short-sighted thinking.

No matter where we find ourselves, we must always remember to go back to our foundation in God. Every journey has its challenges, but with God's truth and grace, we can overcome them. Even those who try to use unrighteous means like magic or rituals cannot truly succeed, for they will ultimately face the consequences of turning away from God.

I am still on the subject named "In the beginning." In every new beginning, let us keep our eyes fixed on God. Pray that His presence, power, and mercy will guide and empower us. If we stay rooted in Him, we will not miss out on the eternal destiny He has prepared for us. May the beauty and glory of God's kingdom rest upon us all, in Jesus' mighty name. Amen.

4

The Rise and Fall of King Saul

In the pages of the King James Bible, the story of King Saul stands as a powerful reminder of how quickly the highest can fall when one forgets their humble beginnings. Saul's journey from obscure youth to anointed king, and ultimately to tragic downfall, offers profound lessons about the importance of maintaining perspective and staying grounded in one's faith.

The narrative of Saul's ascension begins in 1 Samuel, where we are introduced to a young man from the tribe of Benjamin, described as "a choice young man, and a goodly: and there was not among the children of Israel a goodlier person than he" (1 Samuel 9:2). When the Israelites cried out for a king to lead them, the Lord directed the prophet Samuel to anoint Saul, declaring, "Behold the man whom I spake to thee of! this same shall reign over my people" (1 Samuel 9:17).

Saul's humble beginnings as the son of Kish quickly gave way to the trappings of power. Equipped with God's Spirit and the support of the people, Saul emerged as a capable and victorious military leader, securing Israel's borders and conquering its enemies. His early successes and the adulation of the masses appear to have bred in him a dangerous sense of self-reliance and autonomy from God.

It is in this moment of Saul's greatest triumph that the seeds of his downfall begin to take root. Repeatedly, Saul is confronted with opportunities to maintain his humility and obedience to God's commands, but he chooses instead to rely on his wisdom and strength.

The first major misstep occurs when Saul, growing impatient for Samuel's arrival, takes it upon himself to offer a burnt offering in direct violation of God's instructions (1 Samuel 13:8-14). This act of presumption and disobedience elicits a stern rebuke from Samuel, who declares that Saul's kingdom will not endure.

Saul's subsequent reign is marked by a gradual but steady descent into madness, paranoia, and an increasingly erratic disregard for God's ways. His jealousy of David, the young shepherd boy anointed as his successor, leads him on a vengeful campaign of persecution that only serves to further distance him from the divine purpose for which he was chosen.

Ultimately, Saul's tragic downfall can be traced back to his failure to remember his humble beginnings and maintain his dependence on God. As he became intoxicated by power and success, he lost sight of the true source of his authority and anointing. His pride, self-reliance, and disregard for God's commands proved to be his undoing.

The cautionary tale of King Saul serves as a powerful reminder that no matter how high we rise, we must never forget the foundations upon which our lives are built. It is only by preserving a posture of humility, obedience, and steadfast faith that we can hope to fulfill the divine purposes set before us.

In the end, Saul's story stands as a sobering testament to the consequences of forsaking one's beginnings. It is a call to all who aspire to greatness to remain ever mindful of the God who raises and casts down and to guard against the seductive allure of self-reliance and pride. For it is only by remembering our origins and maintaining our dependence on the Almighty that we can truly achieve lasting success and fulfillment.

5

The Cautionary Tale of Ananias and Sapphira

In the book of Acts in the King James Bible, the story of Ananias and Sapphira stands as a sobering warning about the dangers of forgetting one's humble beginnings. This couple's rapid rise and tragic downfall offer a profound lesson about the importance of maintaining integrity, honesty, and unwavering devotion to God's ways.

The backdrop for this account is the burgeoning early Christian church, where the believers were characterized by a remarkable unity and commitment to one another. "And the multitude of them that believed were of one heart and of one soul: neither said any of them that ought of the things which he possessed was his own; but they had all things common" (Acts 4:32).

It was within this spirit of selfless generosity that Ananias and Sapphira made the fateful decision to sell a piece of property and donate the proceeds to the apostles. At first glance, their actions seemed to align with the prevailing ethos of the community. However, as the story unfolds, a darker truth is revealed.

Rather than contributing the full amount they had received from the sale, Ananias and Sapphira conspired to keep back a portion for themselves while presenting the rest as their entire offering. In doing so, they violated the fundamental principle of the early church - that of sacrificial giving and radical honesty.

Their deception was quickly uncovered by the apostle Peter, who confronted Ananias, saying, "Why hath Satan filled thine heart to lie to the Holy Ghost, and to keep back part of the price of the land? 4 Whiles it remained, was it not thine own? and after it was sold, was it not in thine own power? why hast thou conceived this thing in thine heart? thou hast not lied unto men, but unto God.5 And Ananias hearing these words fell, and gave up the ghost: and great fear came on all them that heard these things" (Acts 5:3-5).

Examples of deception include:

Lying on social media about raising money for someone else when you are raising money for yourself. This is a form of fraud and can have serious consequences.

Pretending to like someone when you do not actually like them is another form of deception. This can be hurtful and damaging to relationships.

These examples illustrate how deception can take many forms, but ultimately involve intentionally misleading others for personal gain or advantage. It's important to remember that even seemingly small acts of deception can have significant consequences and go against the principles of honesty and integrity.

However, the story does not end there. When Sapphira, unaware of her husband's fate, arrived sometime later, Peter challenged her with the same question, but her refusal to acknowledge the truth sealed her doom, as she too fell dead before the apostles.

The downfall of Ananias and Sapphira can be traced back to a critical failure - their inability to remember their humble beginnings and the true nature of their newfound faith. In the heady days of the early church, they had lost sight of the radical self-denial and trust in God that had initially defined their journey as believers.

Instead, they succumbed to the temptation of greed and the desire to maintain a veneer of righteousness, while secretly clinging to their own self-interest. By doing so, they betrayed the very spirit of the community they had embraced and incurred the swift judgment of God.

The tragic tale of Ananias and Sapphira serves as a sobering reminder that in the life of faith, there is no room for deception or hypocrisy. God demands our complete honesty, transparency, and devotion - not merely the outward appearance of piety, but the inward transformation of the heart.

Moreover, this account underscores the importance of maintaining a posture of humility and remembering one's beginnings. It is all too easy, during spiritual growth and success, to become complacent and lose sight of the foundational truths that once defined our journey.

The church today would do well to heed the lessons of Ananias and Sapphira. As we strive to build communities of faith, we must guard against the seductive allure of self-interest and the temptation to compromise our integrity. Only by remaining steadfast in our commitment to honesty, generosity, and unwavering devotion to God can we hope to fulfill the divine purpose for which we have been called.

The story of Ananias and Sapphira serves as a stark reminder that even during a vibrant and growing community of faith, the temptation to deceive and prioritize self-interest can quickly lead to devastating consequences. Their tragic downfall underscores the importance of unwavering honesty, integrity, and a willingness to sacrifice for the good of others. It is a cautionary tale for all believers, urging us to remain grounded in the foundational principles of our faith, remembering our humble beginnings, and guarding against the seductive allure of hypocrisy. Only by embracing radical transparency and unwavering devotion to God can we truly live out the transformative power of the Gospel and build a community that reflects the love and grace of our Savior.

6

The Cautionary Tale of Demas

In the annals of the early Christian church, the story of Demas stands as a somber reminder of the perils of forsaking one's spiritual foundations. This once-devoted disciple's rapid rise and tragic downfall offer a profound warning about the importance of maintaining an unwavering commitment to the gospel.

Demas first appears in the New Testament as a faithful companion to the apostle Paul. Mentioned alongside fellow workers like Luke and Aristarchus, Demas is described as a "fellow laborer" who shared in the rigors and joys of Paul's ministry (Colossians 4:14, Philemon 1:24).

In the epistles, Demas is portrayed as a devoted follower of Christ, willing to endure the hardships and persecutions that came with aligning oneself with the nascent Christian movement. His presence alongside Paul, a towering figure of the faith, suggested a promising future in service to the gospel.

However, as the years passed, a dramatic shift began to take place in Demas' life. In his final letter to Timothy, Paul laments, "Demas hath forsaken me, having loved this present world" (2 Timothy 4:10). This stark declaration reveals a troubling reversal – the once-faithful disciple had abandoned his spiritual calling in favor of the allures of the secular world.

What could have led Demas to make such a drastic choice? The text offers no explicit explanation, but the implications are clear. Somewhere along the way, Demas had lost sight of the radical self-denial and unwavering devotion that had once defined his faith. In the face of growing opposition and persecution, he had succumbed to the temptation of comfort, prestige, or perhaps even wealth and status.

At the heart of Demas' downfall lies a critical failure – his inability to remember the humble origins of his spiritual journey. In the heady days of his early discipleship, Demas had likely been captivated by the transformative power of the gospel, the spirit of sacrificial community, and the promise of eternal life. But over time, these foundational truths became obscured by the siren call of the world.

Like Ananias and Sapphira before him, Demas had lost sight of the radical self-denial and trust in God that had once defined his faith. In the pursuit of personal gain and the desire to avoid hardship, he had betrayed the very principles he had once embraced.

The tragic tale of Demas serves as a powerful reminder that in the life of faith, there is no room for compromise or half-measures. God demands our complete devotion, our unwavering commitment to His ways, and our willingness to sacrifice personal comfort for the sake of the gospel.

Moreover, this account underscores the critical importance of maintaining a posture of humility and continually remembering one's spiritual beginnings. It is all too easy, amid success or the allure of the world, to become complacent and lose sight of the foundational truths that once defined our journey.

The church today would do well to heed the lessons of Demas. As we strive to walk the path of discipleship, we must guard against the seductive pull of worldly pleasures and the temptation to compromise our integrity. Only by remaining steadfast in our commitment to Christ, and by constantly renewing our connection to the transformative power of the gospel, can we hope to fulfill the divine purpose for which we have been called.

The story of Demas stands as a sobering reminder that when we forget our humble beginnings, we risk forfeiting the very essence of our faith. May it serve as a clarion call to all who would follow Christ, urging us to cling to the foundational truths that have the power to sustain us, even in the face of the world's most enticing distractions.

The story of Demas serves as a poignant reminder that even those who walk closely with God can be lured away from their faith by the allure of the world. His tragic fall from grace highlights the importance of remembering our spiritual roots and remaining steadfast in our commitment to Christ, even when faced with hardship or temptation. We must guard against the seductive pull of comfort and worldly success, and instead, choose to live lives of unwavering devotion, fueled by the transformative power of the Gospel. Only by holding fast to the foundational truths of our faith can we truly resist the allure of the world and remain faithful to the call of God.

7

The Rise and Fall of the Israelites

The story of the Israelites is one of the most captivating narratives in the annals of human history. From their humble beginnings as a chosen people to their eventual downfall, the Israelites' journey serves as a poignant reminder of the consequences of forsaking one's spiritual foundations.

The Israelites' story began with God's covenant with Abraham, in which He promised to make the patriarch's descendants a great nation and to give them a land of their own (Genesis 12:1-3). This promise was later reaffirmed to Moses, who led the Israelites out of slavery in Egypt and into the Promised Land of Canaan.

Under the leadership of Joshua, the Israelites conquered the land and established a thriving kingdom, governed by a series of judges and, eventually, by a monarchy. Throughout this period, the Israelites' unwavering devotion to God and their commitment to the Mosaic Law were the cornerstones of their identity and success.

However, as the Israelites settled in the Promised Land, a subtle transformation began to take place. The once-humble people became enamored with the trappings of power and influence, yearning for a strong central government like the neighboring nations.

This desire for a king, expressed in 1 Samuel 8, marked a turning point in the Israelites' history. Though God warned them of the consequences of such a choice, the people persisted, and Saul was anointed as the first king of Israel.

The installment of a monarchy ushered in a new era for the Israelites, one that would ultimately lead to their downfall. As the kings of Israel and Judah rose and fell, the people became increasingly distracted by the lure of worldly power and the temptation to emulate the pagan cultures around them.

Time and again, the prophets of God would call the Israelites back to their covenant roots, urging them to remember the mighty acts of deliverance that had defined their past. Yet, too often, the people turned a deaf ear, choosing instead to embrace the seductive ways of the world.

The Israelites' gradual drift from their spiritual foundations had catastrophic consequences. The northern kingdom of Israel fell to the Assyrian Empire in 722 BCE, and the southern kingdom of Judah was later conquered by the Babylonians in 586 BCE.

These events marked the end of the Israelites' autonomy and the beginning of a long period of exile and subjugation. The people who had once been a beacon of hope and a living testament to God's power had become a shadow of their former selves, having forsaken the very tenets that had once defined their identity.

The rise and fall of the Israelites serve as a cautionary tale for the church today. As the people of God, we too are susceptible to the allure of worldly power and the temptation to compromise our spiritual foundations.

Just as the Israelites were called to remember their deliverance from Egypt and their covenant with God, the church must remain vigilant in safeguarding its heritage and its devotion to the gospel. We must resist the urge to conform to the values of the surrounding culture and instead, steadfastly cling to the transformative truth of Scripture.

Only by maintaining a posture of humility, continually reflecting on our spiritual origins, and submitting to the sovereign will of God can we hope to avoid the pitfalls that befell the Israelites. In doing so, we can become a beacon of hope and a living testimony to the power of a faith that transcends the passing fancies of the world.

The story of the Israelites serves as a profound reminder that when we forget our beginnings, we risk losing the very essence of our identity and our purpose. May it inspire us to remain ever vigilant, keeping our eyes fixed on the eternal truths that have the power to sustain us, even in the face of the most alluring distractions.

8

The Rise and Fall of Solomon

The reign of King Solomon stands as one of the most remarkable and complex chapters in the history of ancient Israel. From the heights of his wisdom and prosperity to the depths of his moral decline, Solomon's story serves as a poignant reminder of the consequences of forsaking one's spiritual foundations.

Solomon's ascension to the throne was marked by a divine blessing and a promising future. As the son of King David, the greatest of Israel's monarchs, Solomon inherited a kingdom that was unified, prosperous, and revered among the nations.

But it was Solomon's unwavering devotion to God and his humble request for wisdom that truly set the stage for his remarkable reign. In 1 Kings 3, the young king prays to the Lord, asking for an "understanding mind to govern God's people, that he may discern between good and evil." This humble plea was met with God's favor, and Solomon was granted not only unparalleled wisdom but also immense wealth and power.

Under Solomon's leadership, the kingdom of Israel reached new heights of prosperity and prestige. Solomon's wisdom was renowned throughout the ancient world, and his subjects marveled at the grandeur of his court and the splendor of his reign.

The pinnacle of Solomon's achievements was the construction of the magnificent Temple in Jerusalem, a project that solidified Israel's status as the center of worship for the one true God. Solomon's unwavering commitment to the Mosaic Law and his devotion to the Lord seemed to ensure the continued success and spiritual vitality of the kingdom.

However, as Solomon's reign progressed, a troubling pattern began to emerge. The once-humble king became increasingly enamored with the trappings of power and wealth, surrounding himself with a vast harem of foreign wives and accumulating vast riches and material possessions. This shift in priorities, away from a single-minded devotion to God and toward the pursuit of worldly pleasures, ultimately proved to be Solomon's downfall. The biblical account in 1 Kings 11 records how Solomon's foreign wives "turned his heart after other gods," leading him to embrace the worship of pagan deities and abandon the faith of his fathers.

Solomon's moral and spiritual decline had far-reaching consequences for the kingdom of Israel. The unity and prosperity that had characterized his reign began to unravel, and the seeds of division and conflict were sown. After Solomon's death, the kingdom split into the northern kingdom of Israel and the southern kingdom of Judah, setting the stage for a series of conflicts and conquests that would eventually lead to the downfall of both kingdoms.

The story of Solomon's rise and fall serves as a cautionary tale for modern-day leaders, both in the church and in the secular realm. It reminds us that even the most promising and gifted individuals are susceptible to the temptations of power, wealth, and worldly success, and that forsaking one's spiritual foundations can have devastating consequences.

Just as Solomon was called to remain humble and devoted to the Lord, so too must today's leaders safeguard their hearts and minds against the allure of the material world. They must continually remember their origins, their purpose, and their dependence on the grace of God, lest they too succumb to the traps of pride, greed, and moral compromise.

The story of Solomon's reign is a powerful testament to the importance of maintaining a steadfast commitment to one's spiritual foundations, even in the face of overwhelming success and prosperity. By heeding the lessons of the past, today's leaders can strive to build legacies that are not only marked by worldly achievement but also by a deep and abiding devotion to the eternal principles of God's kingdom.

9

The Urgency of Watchfulness

Matthew 24:44-51 says, "Therefore be ye also ready: for in such an hour as ye think not the Son of man cometh. 45 Who then is a faithful and wise servant, whom his lord hath made ruler over his household, to give them meat in due season? 46 Blessed is that servant, whom his lord when he cometh shall find so doing. 47 Verily I say unto you, That he shall make him ruler over all his goods. 48 But and if that evil servant shall say in his heart, My lord delayeth his coming; 49 And shall begin to smite his fellowservants, and to eat and drink with the drunken; 50 The lord of that servant shall come in a day when he looketh not for him, and in an hour that he is not aware of, 51 And shall cut him asunder, and appoint him his portion with the hypocrites: there shall be weeping and gnashing of teeth."

People who do not remember their beginning are in danger of ending up like the evil servant in the parable who received the reward of eternal condemnation when his Lord returned.

In this parable, the Lord is Jesus who will return one day to give his servants their rewards. This is why the parable warns us not to love sin, but to love to always do the will of God, because no one knows the day when Jesus will return or the day when he or she will die.

Our position should always be one of watching because the Bible says that the thief (Satan) comes to kill, steal, and destroy in John 10:10, but that Jesus came that we might have life.

How do we watch? One way we can watch is to examine our lives daily. Whenever you hear any messages about righteousness, you should ask the Holy Spirit to reveal if the message is addressing something in your life, and he will reveal it to you and give you instructions to follow so that you can correct yourself immediately.

Another way to watch is to be on the lookout daily for the thief (Satan) who enters through our thoughts and shut him out so that he does not enter your "house" (your heart and mind) and destroy it.

Matthew 24:42-43 says "Watch therefore: for ye know not what hour your Lord doth come. 43 But know this, that if the goodman of the house had known in what watch the thief would come, he would have watched, and would not have suffered his house to be broken up."

Solomon's story is a stark reminder that even the most brilliant and successful individuals can fall prey to the allure of worldly power and pleasure. His tragic descent from a wise and righteous king to a man consumed by his desires serves as a warning to all who seek greatness, reminding us that true success lies not in material wealth or worldly acclaim, but in unwavering devotion to God and a commitment to living according to His principles. May we all learn from Solomon's mistakes and strive to maintain a humble heart, a steadfast faith, and a constant awareness of our dependence on God's grace, for only then can we truly build a legacy that endures.

- The Power of Jesus Over Depression: Hope For Depression

- Remember This Word: Walking with God in Righteousness

- The Mind of God Towards Your Service: Fruit

- Come Back To Jesus: Repentance

- Digging Into the Word: Kingdom Lessons 1